PRIZEWINNING
Animals

PRIZEWINNING
CHICKENS

NANCY GREENWOOD

PowerKiDS press

NEW YORK

Published in 2023 by The Rosen Publishing Group, Inc.
29 East 21st Street, New York, NY 10010

First Edition

Portions of this work were originally authored by Jennifer Wendt and published as *Showing Chickens at the Fair*. All new material in this edition authored by Nancy Greenwood.

Editor: Kate Mikoley
Book Design: Andrea Davison-Bartolotta

Photo Credits: Cover andrea lehmkuhl/Shutterstock.com; series art (animal outlines) Picture Window/Shutterstock.com; series art (gold ticket) Mar1kOFF/Shutterstock.com; series art (red ribbon) FMStox/Shutterstock.com; series art (pennant banner, gold ribbon) Tiax/Shutterstock.com; p. 5 MintImages/Shutterstock.com; p. 7 (top left) marilyn barbone/Shutterstock.com; p. 7 (top right) Neil Todd/Shutterstock.com; p. 7 (bottom left) Worraket/Shutterstock.com; p. 7 (bottom right) Muskoka Stock Photos/Shutterstock.com; p. 9 JuneChalida/Shutterstock.com; p. 11 Kleber Cordeiro/Shutterstock.com; p. 13 narikan/Shutterstock.com; p. 15 Dennis van de water/Shutterstock.com; p. 17 Helene Woodbine/Shutterstock.com; p. 18 Aksenova Natalya/Shutterstock.com; p. 19 Oleg Elkov/Shutterstock.com; p. 21 Christin Lola/Shutterstock.com.-

Library of Congress Cataloging-in-Publication Data

Names: Greenwood, Nancy, author.
Title: Prizewinning chickens / Nancy Greenwood.
Description: New York : PowerKids Press, [2023] | Series: Prizewinning
    animals | Includes index.
Identifiers: LCCN 2021040153 | ISBN 9781538386224 (set) | ISBN
    9781538386231 (library binding) | ISBN 9781538386217 (paperback) | ISBN
    9781538386248 (ebook)
Subjects: LCSH: Chickens–Showing–Juvenile literature.
Classification: LCC SF483 .G74 2023 | DDC 636.508/11–dc23
LC record available at https://lccn.loc.gov/2021040153
Manufactured in the United States of America

CPSIA Compliance Information: Batch #CSPK23. For Further Information contact Rosen Publishing, New York, New York at 1-800-237-9932.

Find us on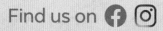

CONTENTS

OFF TO THE FAIR 4

CHOOSING A CHICKEN 6

TAKE CARE OF YOUR CHICKEN. 8

TEAMWORK WINS THE PRIZE. 10

GET READY FOR THE SHOW 12

BATH TIME!. 14

THE BIG DAY. 16

TIME FOR THE SHOW. 18

TIME TO GO!. 20

GLOSSARY 22

FOR MORE INFORMATION. 23

INDEX 24

Off to THE FAIR

The fair is packed with fun things to do, from riding the Ferris wheel to watching people present their animals at shows. You can show your animal at the fair too!

Cows and horses are common animals shown at fairs. Chickens are shown at many fairs too. If you have a chicken, you might want to enter it in a show. Showing animals is hard work, but with time and practice you can make your chicken a prizewinner!

Does your family have chickens? If so, maybe you can show one at a local fair.

Choosing
A CHICKEN

There are many kinds of chickens you can show at the fair. If you don't already have chickens, you can go to a local farm store or search the internet to find a local farm. You'll want to pick a young chick so you can start to train them right away.

Read about different **breeds** before making your choice. You'll also need to decide if you want to show a female chicken (a hen) or a male chicken (a rooster).

Your fair might only allow certain kinds of chickens to be shown. Make sure to check this before getting an animal.

Take Care of YOUR CHICKEN

When you get a chicken to show at the fair, you're in charge of raising it. This means you're **responsible** for its care. Your chicken will need a warm, safe place to live while it's growing. It needs a **coop** or pen large enough for it to get some exercise.

You'll need to feed your chicken a healthy **diet**. Ask your **veterinarian** what the best food is for your type of chicken. With good care, your chicken will grow very fast.

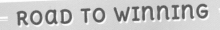

ROAD TO WINNING

Your chicken's bedding should be cleaned daily.

Chickens may eat lots of foods, from oats to worms. A veterinarian will know what's best for your exact chicken.

Teamwork Wins
THE PRIZE

You and your chicken are a team. The more you work with them, the better you'll both do at the fair. Start when your chick is young. Gently pick them up and hold them often.

As your chicken grows, practice taking it out of the pen headfirst. Place one hand over its back and your other hand under its body. Gently hold its legs. Trying this many times will get you and your chicken ready to do this at the fair.

ROAD TO WINNING

You can ask friends or family members to gently pick up and hold your chicken. This will help it get used to being around other people.

Always be gentle when handling your chicken.

Get Ready
FOR THE SHOW

Before the fair, you'll need to know the rules of the show you're taking part in. Read your fair guide to learn what the judges are looking at for your type of chicken.

Be sure your chicken's coop is large enough for their food and water. A few weeks before the fair, practice moving your chicken in and out of the coop. You'll need to be able to do this in front of the judge at the fair.

ROAD TO WINNING

Make sure your chicken has had all the **vaccinations** and blood tests it needs to be able to **compete** at the fair. Keep the records so you can show the fair **officials**.

Practice anything you might need to do with your chicken before the day of the fair. You don't want your chicken dealing with any surprises on the big day!

Bath
TIME!

It can take at least a day for your chicken to dry completely, so give them a bath a few days before the fair. Dip your chicken in warm water with some gentle shampoo, wipe gently, and then rinse. Dry them carefully with a towel.

Depending on your chicken's breed, you can use a comb or brush to fluff its feathers. A toothbrush works great for cleaning a chicken's feet. Some people use baby oil to make their chicken's feet shine.

ROAD TO WINNING

You can keep your cleaning supplies together in a box. Be sure to include a towel, a washtub, gentle shampoo, a comb or brush, a toothbrush, and a nail file.

Different chickens have different needs. Your veterinarian can help you learn the best ways to clean your animal.

The
BIG DAY

The big day is finally here! Check in with fair officials to find out where you'll be keeping your chicken. Write your name and your chicken's information on a special coop tag. The judges will be looking at this.

Keep the coop clean and check on your chicken often to make sure it has fresh water and food. Chickens can sometimes carry **viruses**, so use your own buckets and scoops from home to water and feed your chicken.

Try not to be too nervous on fair day. You've practiced for this!

17

Time for
THE SHOW

You'll be given a time to show your chicken when you check in on fair day. Don't be late! Clean your chicken's coop and do a quick wipe of your chicken right before you head to the show area.

You'll want to look your best too! Wear a clean shirt and pants and keep your hair neat. You may have to answer some simple questions about your chicken. Make sure you're ready with the answers.

ROAD TO WINNING

Some questions the judge may ask about your chicken are: What does it eat? How old is it? What breed of chicken is it?

comb

wattle

A judge may ask you to name and point out certain parts of your chicken. Make sure you know the different parts, such as the wattle and the comb.

Time
TO GO!

Whether you and your animal win or not, showing your chicken at the fair is lots of fun. You get to meet new people, learn more about your animal, and gain skills to help you at the next fair.

Remember to clean up your area when the fair is over. Be sure to thank everyone who has helped you take care of your chicken during the fair. Gather your supplies and your chicken. Then it's time to head home!

ROAD TO WINNING

You may need to **quarantine** your chicken when you take it home. It may have picked up a virus from being around other chickens, and it could make your other animals at home sick.

Winners at animal shows often win ribbons. A blue ribbon usually means first place!

GLOSSARY

breed: A group of animals that share features different from other groups of the kind.

compete: To try to win a contest with others.

coop: A small building where chickens are kept.

diet: The food an animal eats.

official: A person who has a position of authority in a company, organization, or government.

quarantine: To keep a person or animal away from others to stop the spread of an illness.

responsible: Having the job or duty of dealing with or taking care of something or someone.

vaccination: A shot that keeps a person or animal from getting a certain sickness.

veterinarian: A doctor who is trained to treat animals.

virus: A very tiny thing that can cause illness when it enters the body.

FOR MORE INFORMATION

BOOKS

Colella, Jill. *Let's Explore Eggs!* Minneapolis, MN: Lerner Publications, 2021.

De la Bédoyère, Camilla. *From Egg to Chicken*. London, England: QEB Publishing, 2019.

London, Martha. *Baby Chickens*. Minneapolis, MN: Cody Koala, 2021.

WEBSITES

Chickens
www.dkfindout.com/us/animals-and-nature/domesticated-animals/chickens/
Learn more about chickens on this interactive page.

4-H
4-h.org
Through hands-on projects, 4-H encourages children to learn new skills, including caring for and showing chickens.

The Pioneer Chicks
www.thepioneerchicks.com/category/chickens/
This website has tons of articles about raising and showing chickens.

INDEX

B
bedding, 8
breeds, 6, 14, 18

C
cleaning, 8, 14, 15, 16, 18, 20
comb, 19
coops and pens, 8, 10, 12, 16, 18
cows, 4

D
diet, 8, 9

F
fair guide, 12

H
hen, 6
horses, 4

J
judges, 12, 16, 18, 19

R
ribbons, 21
rooster, 6

S
supplies, 14, 20

V
vaccinations, 12
veterinarian, 8, 9, 15
virus, 16, 20

W
wattle, 19